Drawing Shape by Shape

Drawing Shape by Shape

Create Cartoon Characters with
Circles, Squares & Triangles

Chris Hart Books

New York

Chris Hart Books

An imprint of
Sixth&Spring Books
161 Avenue of the Americas
New York, NY 10013

Editorial Director
JOY AQUILINO

Senior Editor
MICHELLE BREDESON

Editorial Assistant
ALEXANDRA JOINNIDES

Art Director
DIANE LAMPHRON

Book Design
NANCY SABATO
EMILY JONES

Vice President, Publisher
TRISHA MALCOLM

Production Manager
DAVID JOINNIDES

Creative Director
JOE VIOR

President
ART JOINNIDES

chrishartbooks.com

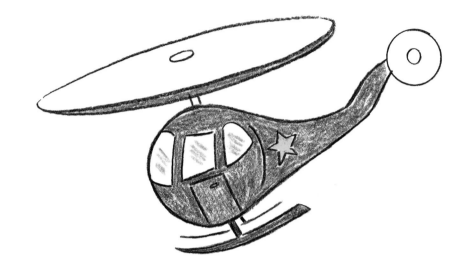

Library of Congress Control
Number: 2011942092

ISBN: 978-1-936096-41-1

What's Inside

Let's get Started

Welcome, artists!

In this book, I'm going to show you the easiest way to draw.

By starting with just a circle (or a square or triangle) and

adding to it bit by bit, you will be able to draw all

kinds of cute animals and crazy cartoon characters.

All you need to start is a pencil and some paper. You can use

a drawing pad or sketchbook or just some scrap paper.

It's easy to make mistakes when you're drawing.

To get rid of any errors, just rub them out with an eraser.

If you need a little help drawing your circles, squares,

and triangles, there are templates in the back of the book.

Just cut them out with scissors (ask Mom or Dad to help)

and trace around the shapes with your pencil.

To add some color to your finished drawing, you can use crayons,

markers, or colored pencils, like I did for this book. Remember that the

more you practice drawing, the easier it will get. So grab a

pencil and some paper and start creating!

Happy Drawing!
Chris Hart

DRaw a CIRCLE

Can you draw a ? Then you can draw anything!

Would you like to draw a playful 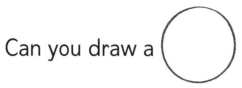? How about a

 from another planet? Or a swashbuckling ?

You'll learn how to draw all of them,

plus a beautiful , a wiggly ,

and lots more cool characters and silly animals.

Perky Panda

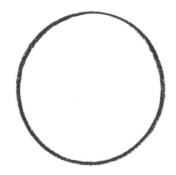 

feathered friend

black belt

bashful puppy

PiLot boy

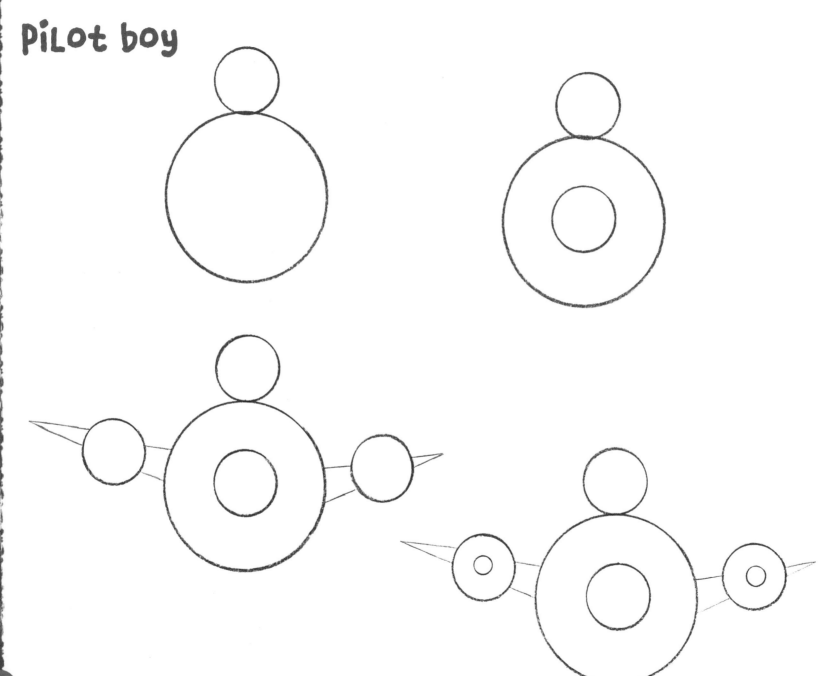

15

HUNGRY MOUSE

martian

football PLayer

feeling blue

MERMaiD

Hot air balloon

ant

yo-yo boy

brown bear

goofy gorilla

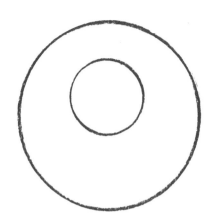

SUPER villain

hatching chick

friendly dinosaur

something fishy

mad scientist

OSTRICH

aLiEN SPaceSHiP

Sea Lion

zebra

cute Kitten

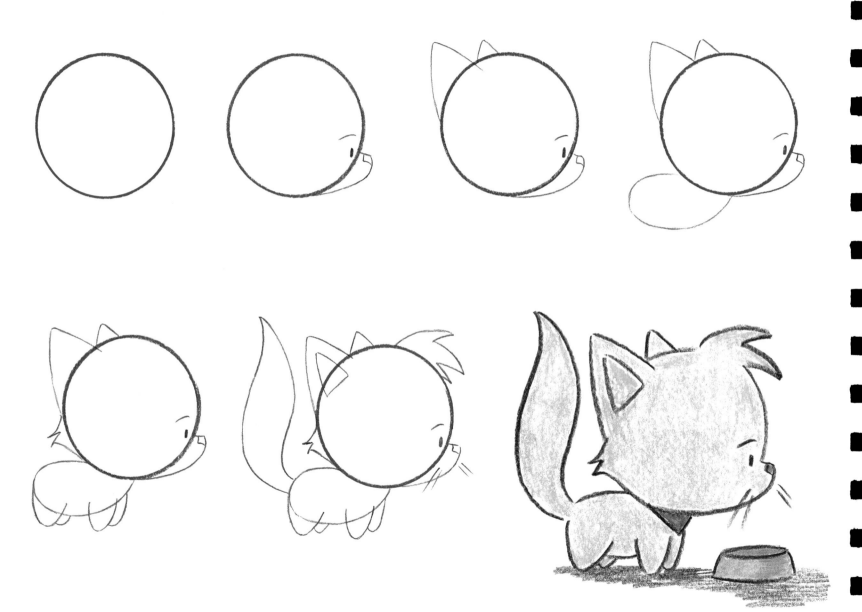

Hula-Hoop Girl

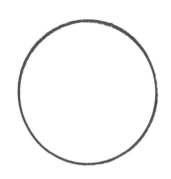

SPINNING out of CONTROL!

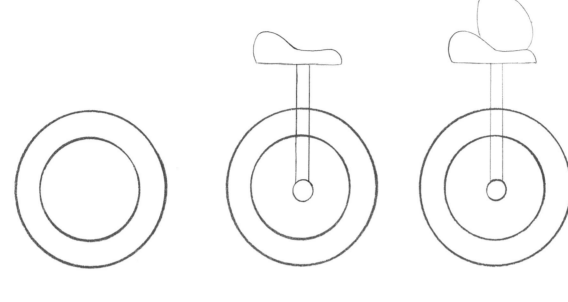

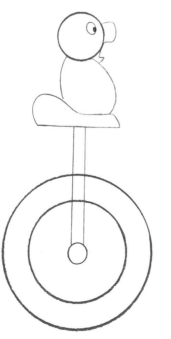

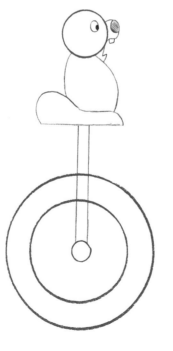

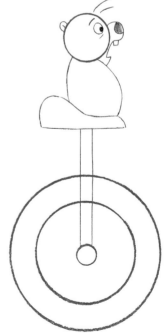

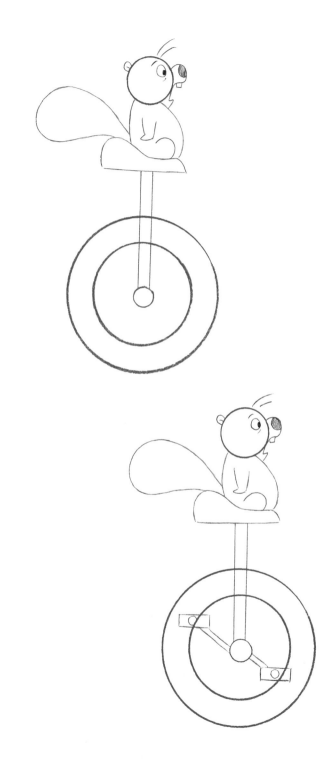

41

manga boy

KOOKY CREATURE

SLy SHARK

LittLe Doggy

SMILING SUN

eagle

best friends

caterpillar

master chef

PRO WRESTLER

raccoon bandit

Just Ducky

ogre

KANGAROO AND JOEY

57

abominable snowman

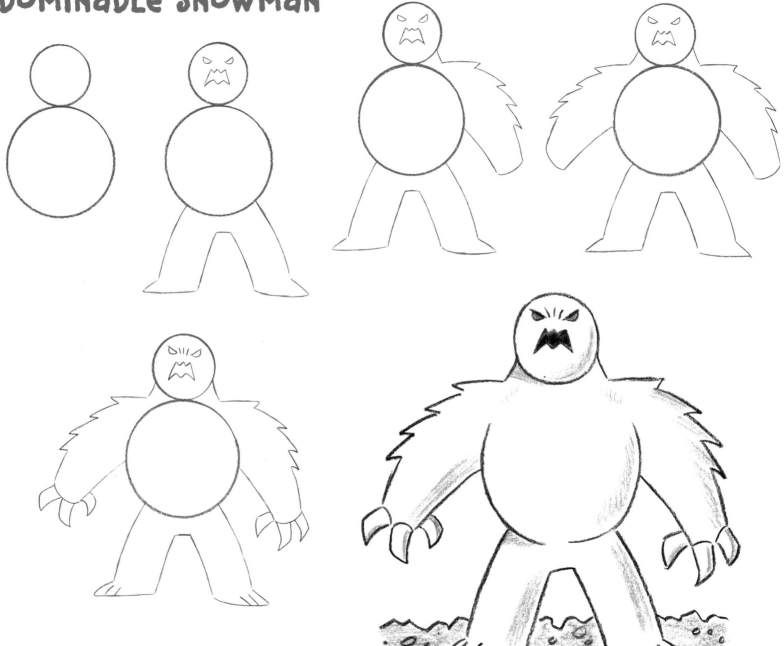

meek mouse

angry bull

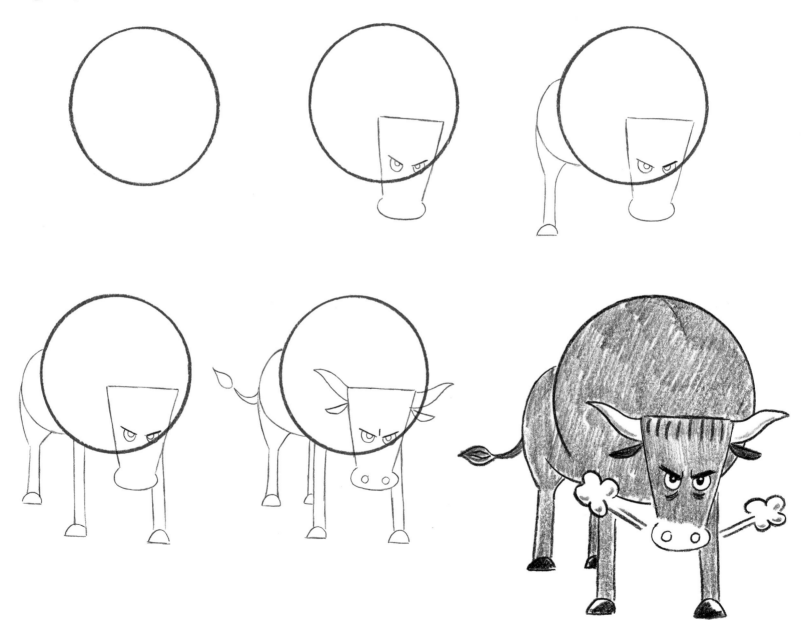

SHy Guy

guarD DOG

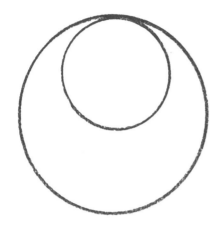

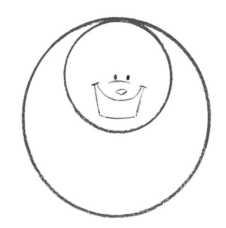

Pirate

Hovering Helicopter

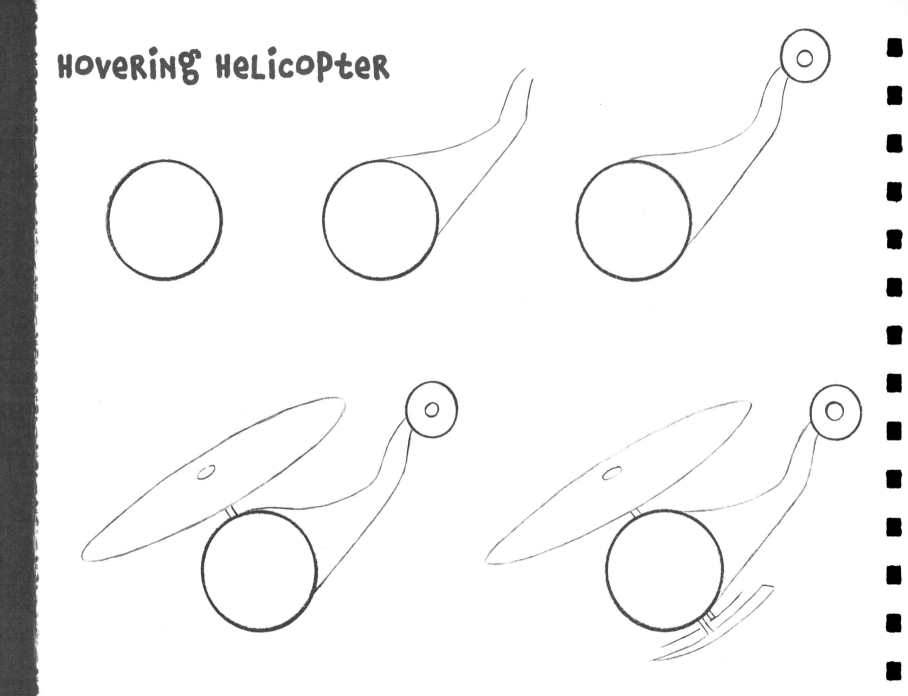

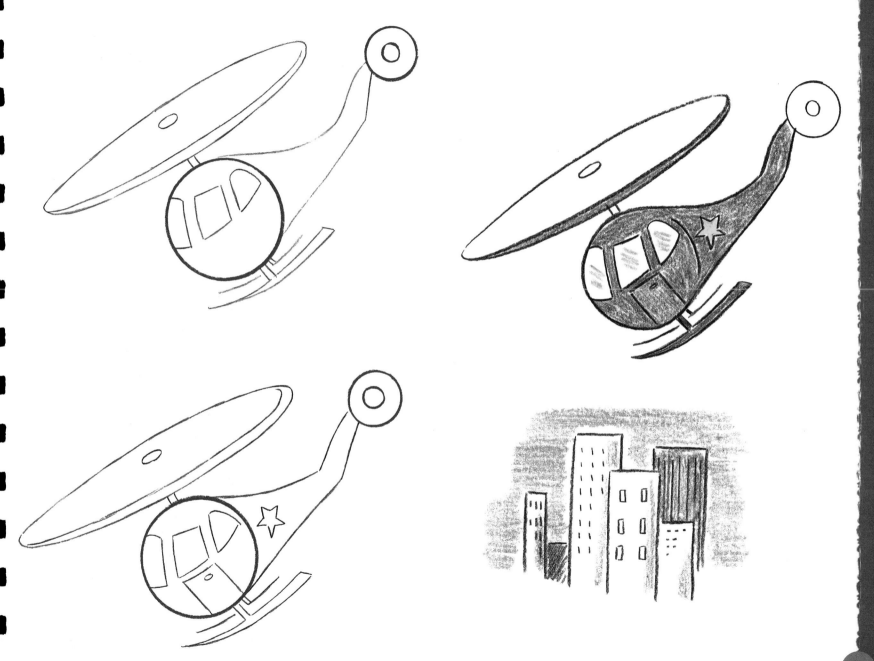

bumbling burglar

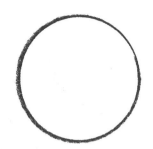

octopus

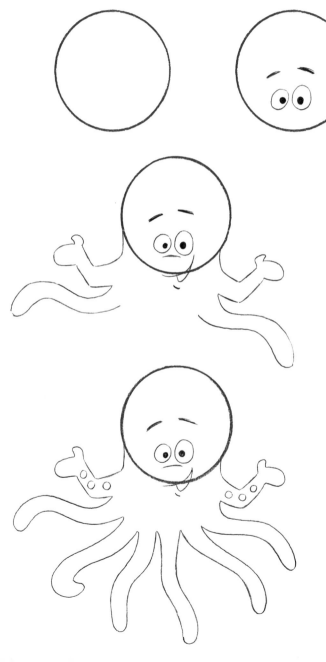

Draw a Square

Now let's see what you can make out of a ☐ ! How about a

cuddly 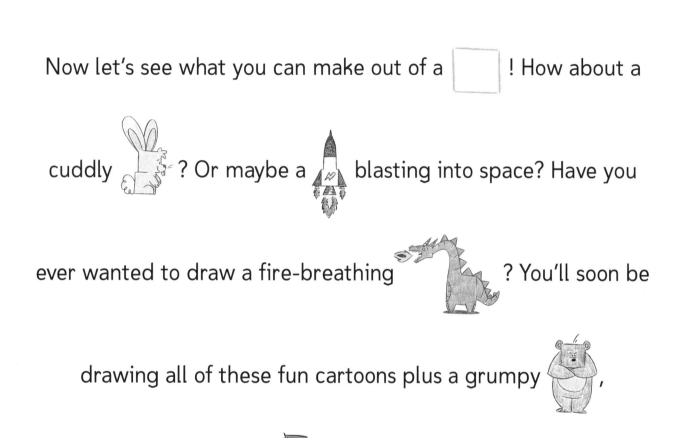 ? Or maybe a blasting into space? Have you

ever wanted to draw a fire-breathing ? You'll soon be

drawing all of these fun cartoons plus a grumpy ,

a caped , and so much more!

Puzzled Penguin

a HORSE (of course)

Pretty in Pink

Hopping Along

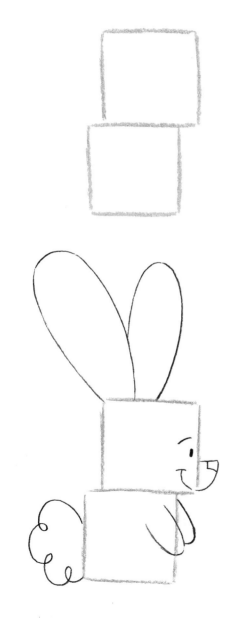

baseball boy

ELf

dainty deer

T. Rex

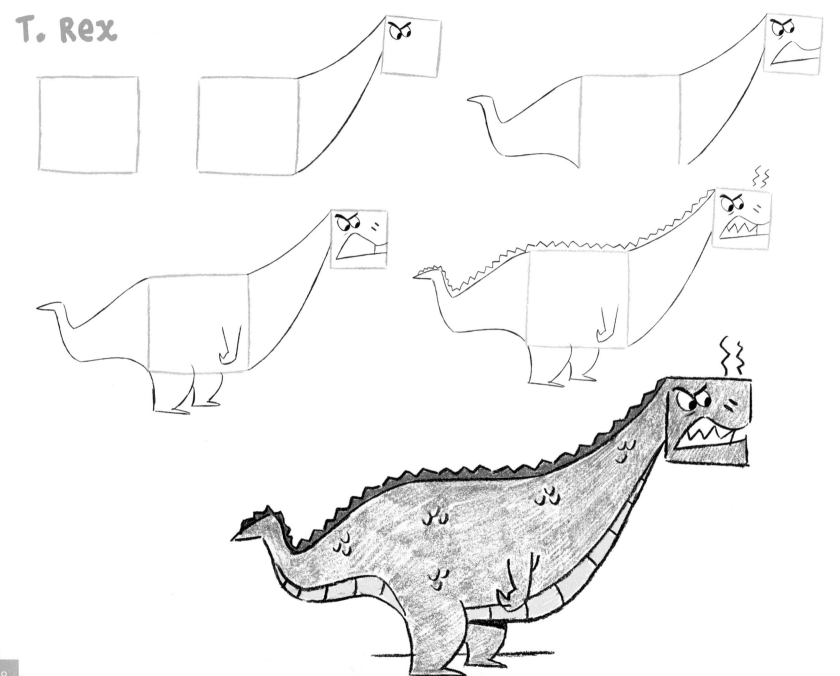

boy with glasses

trailing behind

Home Sweet Home

freckle face

Little Robot

PLAYFUL PUPPY

knight in armor

vampire

boy astronaut

Sheriff of the town

eager beaver

Pink Pig

three-star general

CHiHUAHUA

freight train

bear cub

baby gator

MR. MOUSE

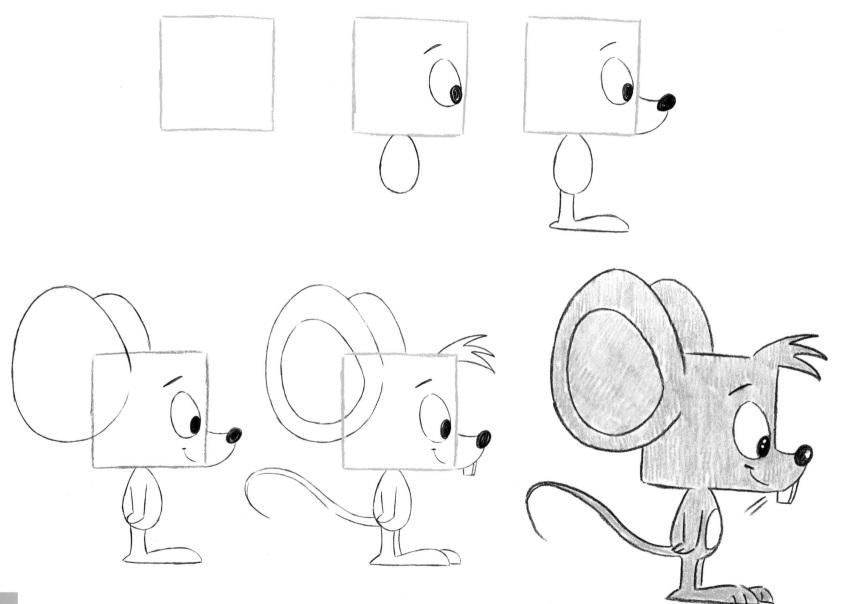

green-haired girl

CRIME fighter

ROCKET SHIP

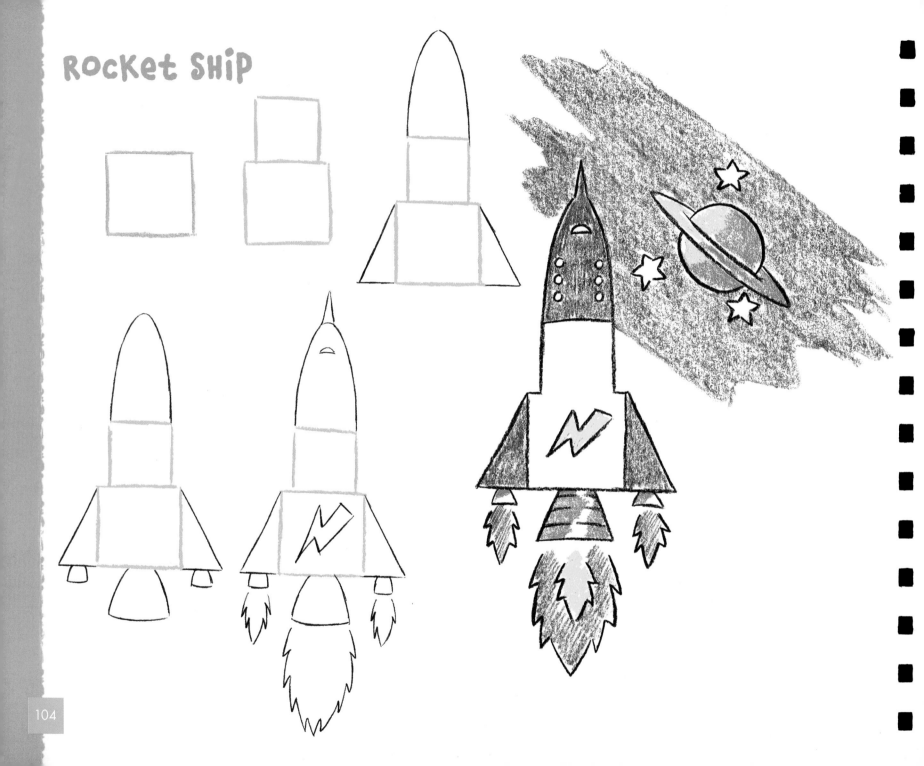

"Fetch!"

KINDLY KING

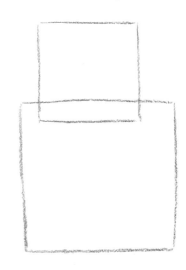

fire-breathing dragon

black cat

GRUMPY GRIZZLY

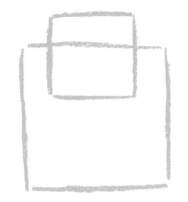

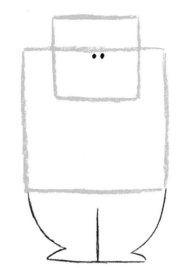

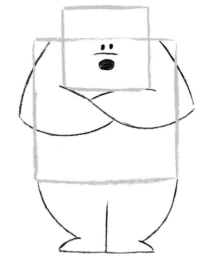

fairy-tale castle

SuRPRiSeD SNaiL

friendly lion

beach boy

Peaceful Pachyderm

spotted tortoise

monKeying around

117

MR. POLICEMAN

Hippo

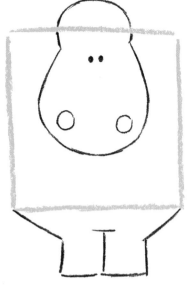

Palomino Horse

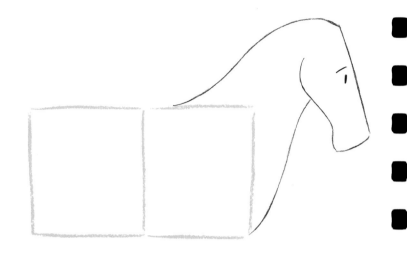

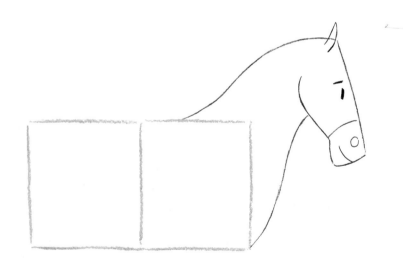

121

CRANKY COW

giraffe

123

cement truck

FRANKENSTEIN'S MONSTER

Jet airplane

WHale

Draw a Triangle

Even a  can become lots of different wacky characters

and cute animals! Would you like to draw a sweet little  ?

How about a  with magical powers? Or a futuristic  ?

You'll soon be able to draw all of them, plus a prickly

 , a kooky  , and lots more

funny characters and crazy animals.

Daffy Dog

Little Piggy

boy next door

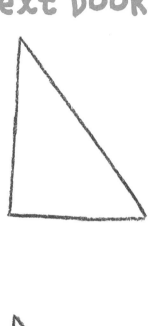

Lioness

busy beaver

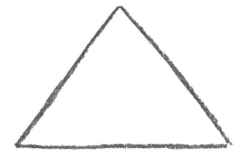

134

wizard

flower and bee

Snack time

Science Guy

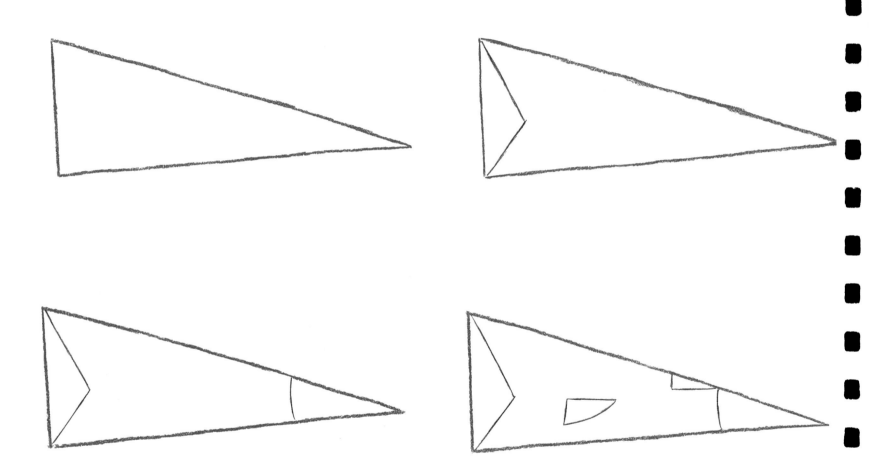

Silly Snail

wicked witch

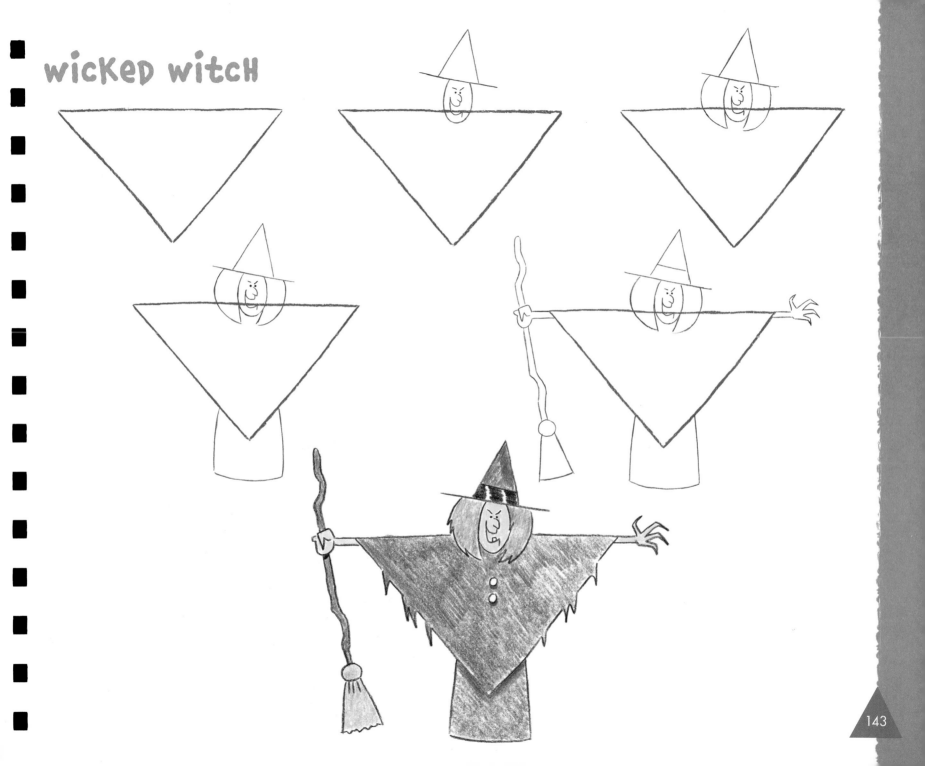

scared as a mouse

cool guy

 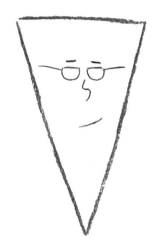 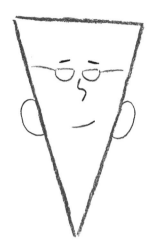

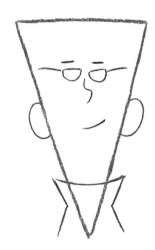  

145

Sea turtle

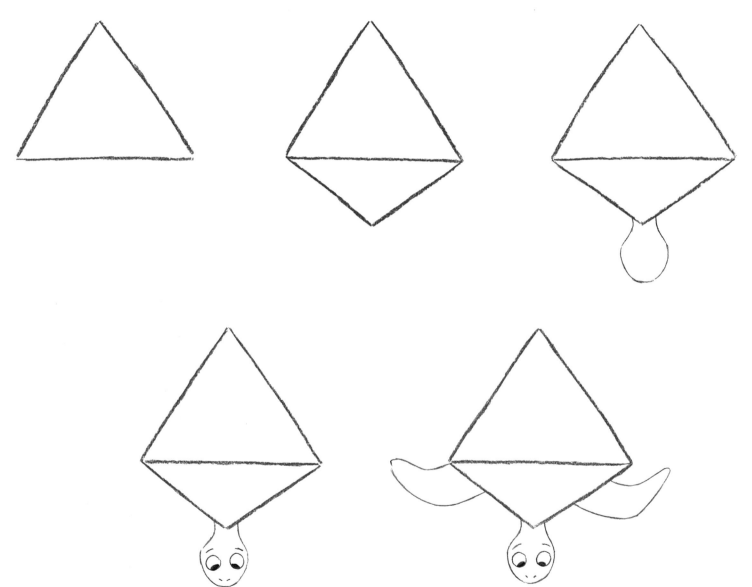

147

DACHSHUND

skateboard boy

PORCUPINE

evil queen

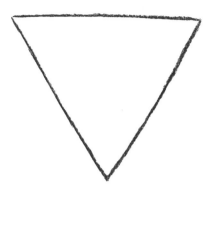
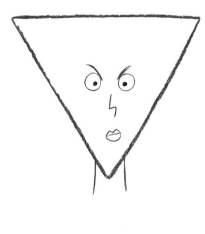

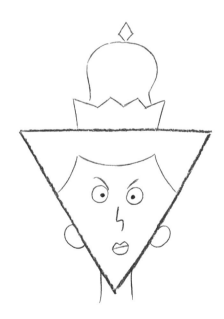
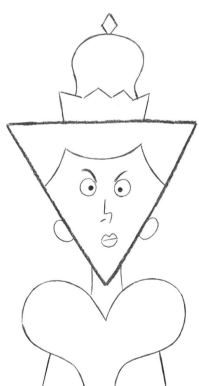

151

REINDEER

bLuebiRD

temper tantrum

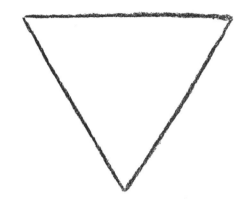 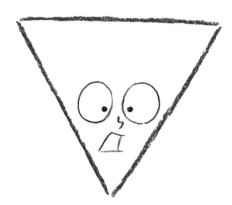 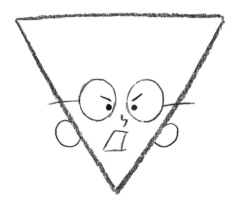

154

walrus

ice cream cone

Sinister Snake

cheerful boy

going ape!

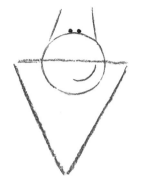
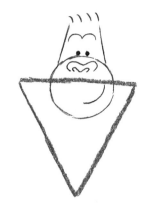

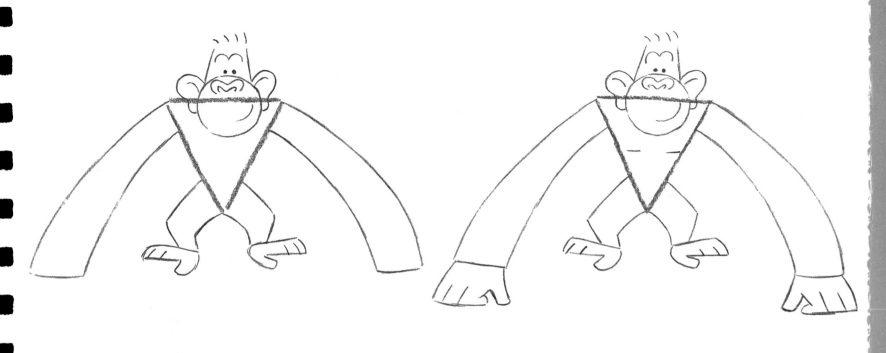

FRENCH MAN

PeLiCaN

emperor

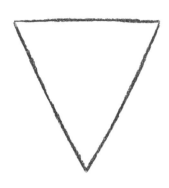

gentle giraffe

MASKED HERO

166

Persian Kitten

DOPEY DRAGON

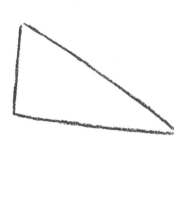

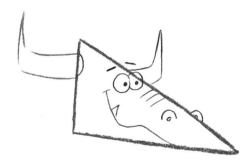

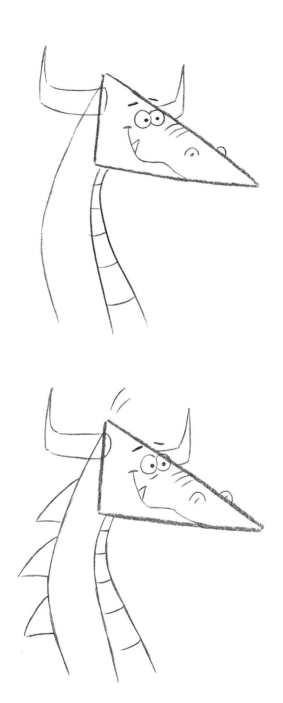

SHOPPING DAY

HORSe HeaD

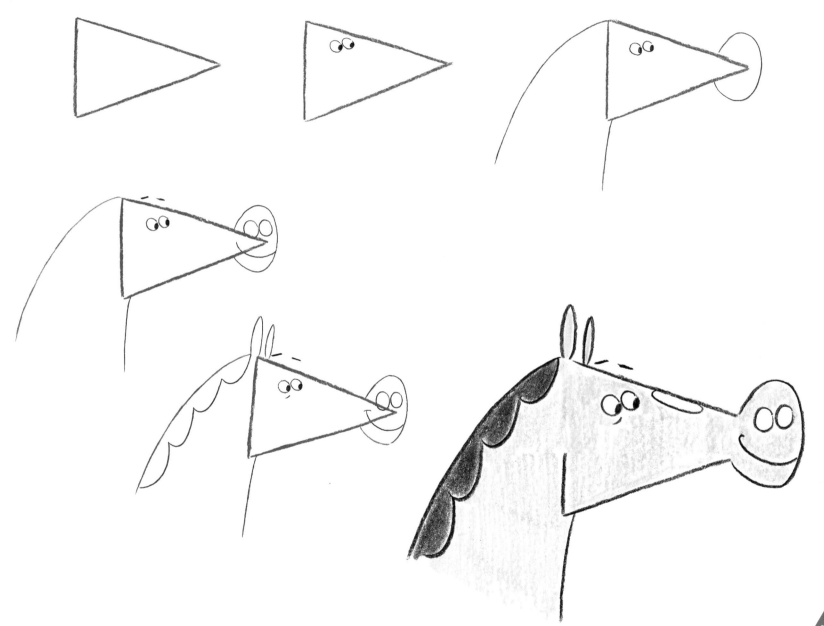

guy with glasses

yeti

timid tiger

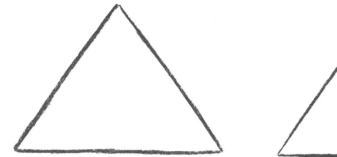  

flying fairy

mega Robot

to the Rescue!

futuRIstic boy

BARRACUDA

SCARY DINOSAUR

caveman

PRetty PuPPy

big fish

teePee

Nice Gnome

Put It All Together!

Now that you can draw with circles, squares,

and triangles, try using all three shapes in one drawing!

INDEX

Looking for your favorite animal or character? Check the alphabetical list to see which page it's on.

Now that you can draw with simple shapes, what's next?

Cut & Trace Templates

If you need a little help drawing circles, squares, and triangles, just cut around the shapes on this page and trace. You'll be off to a great start!